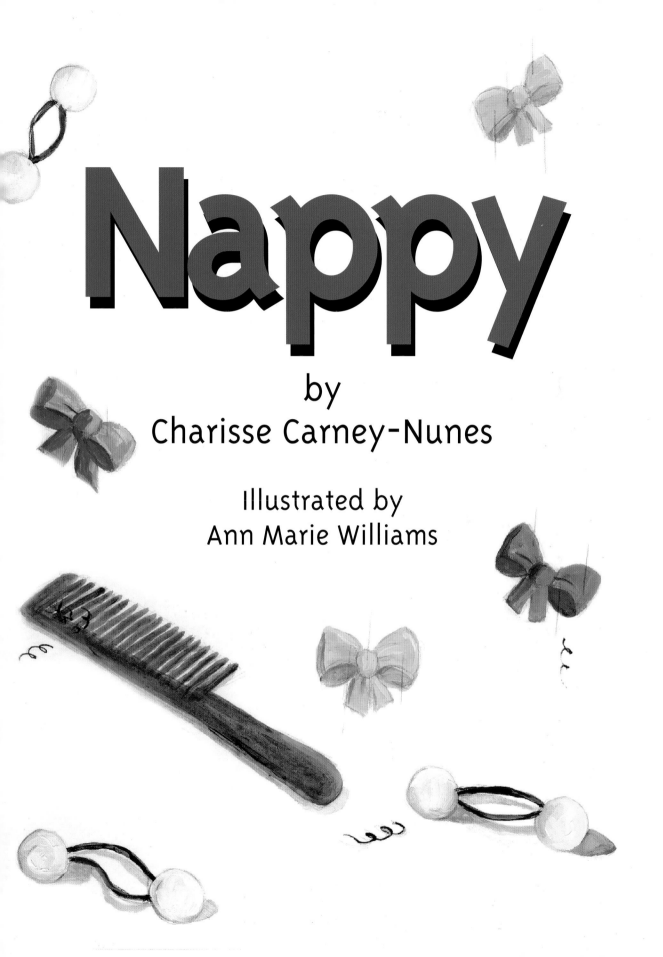

Nappy

by
Charisse Carney-Nunes

Illustrated by
Ann Marie Williams

Published by Brand Nu Words LLC

To order additional copies of this book contact:

Brand Nu Words
1314 Fairmont Street NW
Washington, DC 20009
www.BrandNuWords.com
1-202-387-1314

ISBN: 978-0-9748142-1-6

Library of Congress Control Number: 2005906741

Second Edition: June 2008

Printed in China

Little girl...

Our hair is...
super-
nappturally
NAPPY

It's
super-
abundantly
NAPPY

It's super-eminently
NAPPY

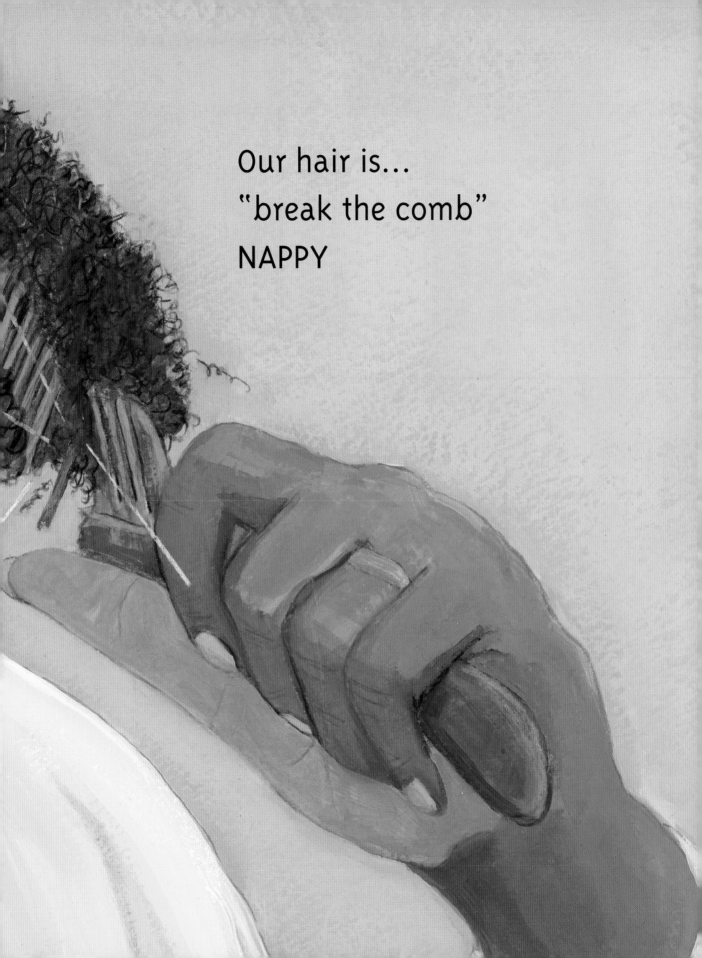

Our hair is...
"break the comb"
NAPPY

..."run out the chair" NAPPY

..."scalp just can't bear" NAPPY

...."scream for a perm" NAPPY
...."perm 'til you burn" NAPPY

Our hair is...
  PULL...ouch
    TWIST...ouch
      TURN...ouch
    KINK...ouch
  COIL...ouch
    SNAP...ouch
  CRACK...ouch
  POP...ouch NAPPY!!!

But girl,
God didn't give us nothing
we couldn't handle.

It's "Underground Railroad" NAPPY

Harriet Tubman
A PASSAGE TO FREEDOM

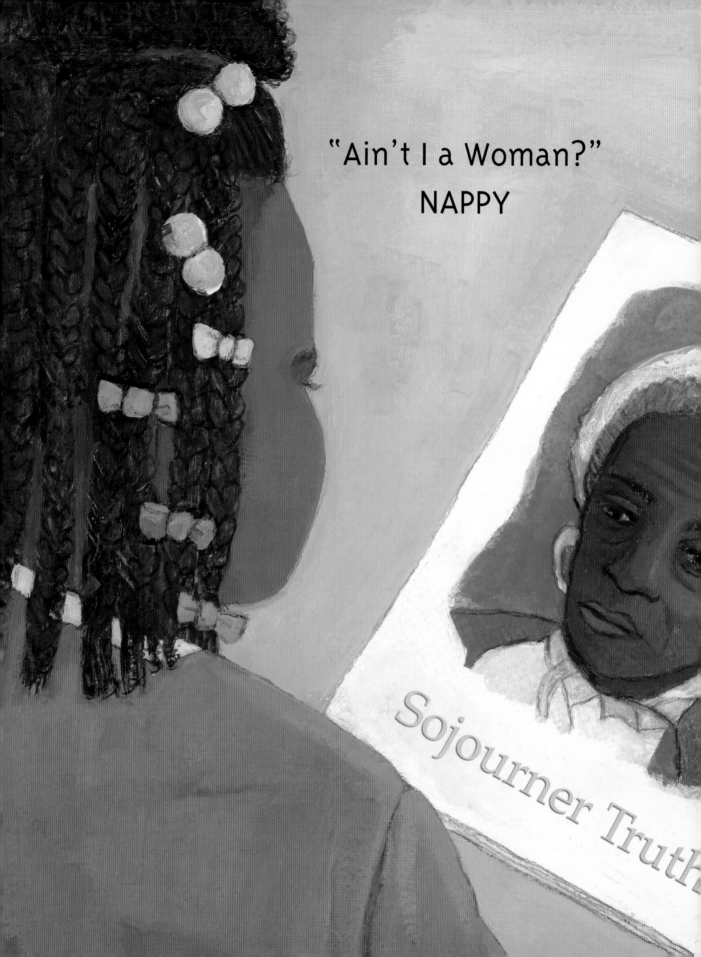

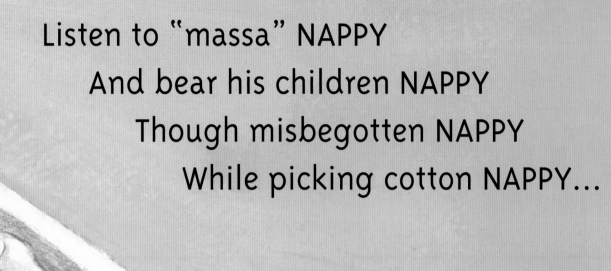

Listen to "massa" NAPPY
And bear his children NAPPY
Though misbegotten NAPPY
While picking cotton NAPPY...

Our hair is Harriet Tubman
Sojourner Truth
Mary McLeod
Rosa Parks
Ella Baker
Josephine Baker
Zora Neale Hurston
Ida B. Wells
Sonia Sanchez
and
Angela Davis
...NAPPY.

'Cause girl,
God didn't give us nothing
we couldn't handle.

Ella Baker was an extremely important person in the Civil Rights Movement in America. Yet, today, most Americans do not even know who she was. Ella lived for many years in New York City where she fought for freedom and justice for African Americans and worked with many organizations, including the National Association for the Advancement of Colored People (NAACP). Martin Luther King was so impressed with her, that he invited Ella to move to Atlanta to help him with his work in the Civil Rights Movement. She later moved to North Carolina where she helped students start the Student Nonviolent Coordinating Committee (SNCC), an organization that encouraged women, the young, and the poor to become leaders and to work for civil rights. Over the years, Ms. Baker worked with many men who were not used to her feisty, spunky and independent way of doing things. Ms. Baker continued to fight for freedom until she died in 1986 at the age of 83.

Josephine Baker, born in 1906, was a famous African-American dancer, actress, and singer who later became the most popular American entertainer living in France. Her shows were controversial; she may be best known for dancing in a skirt made out of bananas and performing with her pet leopard, Chiquita. Off stage, Josephine fought for equality. She refused to perform in America unless audiences contained both Blacks and Whites. She adopted twelve orphans from different cultural backgrounds, calling them her "Rainbow Tribe." During World War II, Josephine tried to help her adopted country, France, resist control by the Nazis. She died in 1975 just when her career was on the upswing again.

Mary McLeod Bethune is one of the most important teachers in American History. She opened a school for African-American girls in 1904, during a time when very few African Americans could read or write. Her students had to use boxes and packing crates for desks, and charcoal for pencils. Years later as her school grew, it joined with another school for African-American boys, and Bethune-Cookman College was formed. It is still educating students in Daytona Beach, Florida, today! Mary was also a political activist. She often visited the White House and was an advisor to four U.S. Presidents on issues concerning education and children. In 1935, she started the National Council of Negro Woman, an organization that today joins together hundreds of thousands of Black women across the world. Mary McLeod Bethune died in 1955, and is buried on the campus of Bethune-Cookman College.

Angela Davis has been a student, teacher, author, philosopher, "radical" activist, and political candidate. She was active in political causes where she grew up (in Birmingham, Alabama), but became famous in 1969 when she was removed from her teaching position in California because instead of being a Republican or a Democrat, she was a member of the Communist party. She became notorious when she was accused of helping a prisoner break out of jail. Even though she was cleared of all charges, some people best remember her for this incident. Angela reclaimed her job as a college professor, co-founded an organization called the National Alliance Against Racism and Political Repression, and today continues her life-long struggle against oppression.

Zora Neale Hurston was a writer who studied people—the way they live, behave, talk, and the things that they like to do. Today she is sometimes called the "literary grandmother" of Black women authors; however, during much of her life, her work did not receive the recognition it deserved. She was an important part of the Harlem Renaissance—a time in the 1930s when Blacks formed a creative community in Harlem, New York City, around art, music, writing, and social thoughts about civil rights and equality. Zora was born in 1891 and died in 1960 without a lot of recognition. In recent years, there has been renewed interest in her work. In 2005, Oprah Winfrey produced a television movie starring Halle Berry, based on Zora's most important novel, "Their Eyes Were Watching God."

Rosa Parks had a life-long career in Civil Rights. In her early days she worked on issues like making sure Black children received a good education and that Black people were free to exercise their right to vote. Rosa Parks is most famous for refusing when a bus driver in Montgomery, Alabama, ordered her to give up her seat to a White person on December 1, 1955. The police arrested her because her action broke the law that required Blacks to stand when there were not enough seats on the bus for Whites. Rosa's arrest outraged the community of Blacks in Montgomery. As a result, they refused to spend their money to ride any buses until the company changed its rules. Most people agree that Rosa's act of courage was the beginning of the Civil Rights Movement in America, and that it led to the end of laws that required things to be separate for Black and White people. Rosa Parks died in 2005 at the age of 92.

Sonia Sanchez is one of today's most popular poets. She was born in 1934 in Birmingham, Alabama. Her mom died while she was still a baby. When Sonia was nine years old, her dad took the family to New York City. Sonia studied politics and writing in college, and became very active in the Civil Rights Movement in the 1960s. She published poetry about the conflicts between Black and White people, men and women, and about people from different cultural backgrounds. Sonia has written more than a dozen books of poetry, many children's books, and several plays. As a lecturer, she has spoken at more than 500 universities across the world. She has won countless awards for her work and for her community service. Sonia still lives in Philadelphia where she was a college professor for more than 20 years. She continues her work today.

Harriet Tubman is probably the most well known of America's former slaves. Even though we all know her name, how much do Americans really know about Harriet Tubman? She was born in 1819 or 1820 as a slave. Both of her parents were brought to this country from Africa, so she was purely of African descent. Even as a young girl, Harriet was always ready to stick up for somebody else. In her early teens, an overseer struck her on the head with a two-pound weight as she blocked a doorway to protect another field hand from the angry overseer. Although she recovered, for the rest of her life she continued to suffer "sleeping spells," which meant she would fall unconscious for long periods of time. When Harriet was 29 years old, she heard a rumor that she, her husband, and other slaves on the Maryland plantation where she lived were going to be sold and taken further into the South. She ran away one night and sought the help of a friendly White woman whom she had met while working in the fields. The woman took Harriet into her house for the night, and told her which way to travel through the woods to another safe house. When Harriet arrived at the next house, another family fed her and drove her further north in a covered wagon as she hid under a blanket. During her long escape to freedom in Philadelphia, Harriet stopped at many more safe houses and was hidden in a haystack, on a farm, and even in a potato hole. This was the beginning of Harriet's journeys to and from the North and South along the Underground Railroad. The Underground Railroad was not a real railroad, of course. It was a system of friendly people who provided safe places where slaves could rest and get help as they fled from slavery in the South to freedom in the North. Harriet became the Underground Railroad's most famous "conductor," making 19 trips between the North and South, bringing more than 300 slaves to freedom. She made her last trip in 1860 when she led her 70-year-old parents all the way to Canada and freedom. During the Civil War, Harriet joined the army and served as a spy and a nurse for Union soldiers. In later years, she spent her time helping educate former slaves and fighting for women's voting rights. She died in 1913 at about 94 years old.

Sojourner Truth fought against slavery and in favor of women's rights. Sojourner, herself, was born a slave in New York in 1797. When she was about 30 years old, New York passed a law freeing its slaves, but she still had to run away to Canada to escape from her master. She returned to New York and began preaching on street corners about religion, freedom, and women's rights. Her speech, "Ain't I a Woman?" was about Black women being included in the movement for women's rights. Sojourner became a famous speaker — hundreds of people followed her wherever she spoke. She made history by winning two famous court cases against prominent Whites. One of those cases ended the practice of segregated streetcars in Washington, DC. During the Civil War, she helped get supplies to Union soldiers, and helped work with former slaves. She died in Michigan in 1883 at about 86 years old.

Ida B. Wells refused to give up her seat on a train in Memphis, Tennessee, seventy-five years before Rosa Parks refused to give up her seat on a bus. The conductor tried to force Ida into the smoking car so that a White man could sit down. She refused to move until the conductor and the baggage man literally picked her up and threw her off of the train. She went back to Memphis and began to write many articles about what happened to her and about the unfair things that happened to other Black people. Because of her writing, life became very dangerous in Memphis, so she moved to Chicago, where she continued to write. There Ida also helped to develop organizations to improve life for African Americans, especially women. In 1930, she made history by running for public office in the state of Illinois. Ida died in 1931 at the age of 69.